UNFROZEN

Unfrozen

Poems of the
West Country

Stephen Allen

First published in the United Kingdom in 2022

by The Hobnob Press,
8 Lock Warehouse, Severn Road, Gloucester GL1 2GA
www.hobnobpress.co.uk

British Library Cataloguing in Publication Data
A catalogue record for this book is available from the British Library

ISBN 978-1-914407-40-6

Typeset in Adobe Garamond Pro 12/14 pt.
Typesetting and origination by John Chandler

Picture Credits

cover Woodminton Down, James Lynch, with permission from the artist

2-3 A very foggy day, Dotun55, creative commons, CC BY-SA 4.0

9 Mistle Thrush, Daniel Cole, with permission from the artist

29 Ancient Yew, Acabashi, Creative commons, CC BY-SA 4.0

44-5 Pike, Jik Jik, creative commons, CC BY-SA 3.0

55 Salisbury Cathedral, John Constable, Victoria and Albert Museum, public domain

68-9 Grazing at dawn, Paul Earle, creative commons, CC0 1.0

Creatures

Owl

At deepest dusk an owl has myth-work to perform
Making low slow progress on stealthy silent wings
To see and hear the tussock underworld and turn
By sleight of flight the nemesis of voles and mice

Its face, a perfect hunting dish for sound and sight
To humans is an eerie source of half-seen ghosts
As its sudden soundless glide across torch beam light
Allows a brief transforming glimpse of another world

Appearing to arise from ancient times of strife
To gladly sit in cautious hearts with iced respect
Confirmed by its shriek at King Duncan's death
An owl is an ally, not a cipher to neglect

At breaking dawn, the favoured owl is barn box bound
An earthy perfect bird and farmers' friend again
Not by day the symbol of the spirit-laden dark
But quiet, bright and lively in its grace-and-favour den

Conservation

From deep within a morning mist
The ruined walls of Teignhead Farm
Provide theatre for a sound
That springs from ground now out of sight
And does not signify alarm
Or throw a caution through the cloud
But brings a pleasing word ashore
Its flutes and burbles penetrate
Far beyond the watery shroud
A note of hope in pure-song form
A curlew calls on Dartmoor

Water memory

A blue-flash bird, then another
Take a centre-line flight along a stream
To a time-entitled food pool and alight
On their bequeathed willow wand and seem
To sense a departure, then discover
The pool has changed but sounds the same
Yet the water's details are not right

Something has altered their only world
Changing its clearwater essence
The smell is a dog's nose different
The fish slime a layer too thick
Their splash has a faint iridescence
And the surface settles too quick

And they know it
Because kingfishers have long water memory
Recent, for the last dip and catch
When the dawn hunger was satisfied
Lifelong, for this brook and this hunting patch
From emerging at egg-break and fledging in burrows
Evolved, adapted, genomic and unlearnable
Since small fish came to live in the shallows

Farthing tail

Dreoilín
The tiny triller
Loved and loathed
Persecuted and misused
Chased on St Stephen's day
Killed by a rough and sorry man
"Give us a penny to bury the wran"
Mindlessly to assuage a superstitious fear
Of bad luck and misfortune in the coming year
Eagle's humiliator
Becoming the King of Birds
Omitted from the "parlement of foules"
Mythic status so confirmed
Spring invigorator
So, no more "jenty hunt" to flee across the field
Forgiven for drumming upon the Irish shield
Celebrated for its famous hearty song
Plucky-bird now can do no wrong
By our coming to appreciate
A scion of our sentiment
Loved and lauded
Farthing tail
Jenny

Colloquium

An arresting sound
Radiates from a dead ash
Bird colloquium
Before the spring dispersal
Of avian lives
As instinctive vows are made
In the super-flock
To survive and multiply
When shadows unlock
Finches in the setting sun
Rise upon the sky

Sole dynamic

Wild hunting balance
Eschews the sentimental
By application

In the free forest
Selfish genes prevail and are
The sole dynamic

Song birds sensing that
Predation is impending
Inevitably

Through the tree tunnel
Natural realpolitik
A goshawk swooping

Unfrozen

Before the first frost of November
In long loose skeins the night-flights alight
Following constellations and magnetic sight
Skimming round time-shaded barrows and mounds
Feathered flocks of Norse-birds return
Redwings and fieldfares with rustling sounds
By hawthorn and rowan are drawn to the ground
They rest and feast in their winter domain
Conditioned and ready to flee in the spring

Who are they?
Perceived as foreign in human ken
A winter Valkyrie, a summer Gaill
On reciprocal roads from south to north
So, where is her home, the waxwing hen?

She follows the stars to find her time
She follows the stars to feel her worth
She follows the stars to feel the earth
Unfrozen at her feet

Soft day

A lake of bright mist
Is oozing through the valley
Trapping the sunrise
It makes superfine drizzle
Ground creatures emerge
Enjoying times of plenty
Mindless of the risk
A flurry of consumption
Easy providence
Under the warm damp blanket
But something watches
The song thrush loves a soft day
Singing and eating

Consequences

For reasons now lost
An elegant equine form
Was carved on the hill

The sun is heating
The denuded ancient stone
Facing the South-West

A Kestrel gliding
On the cusp of hovering
Above the chalk horse
Sees a dragonfly
Quartering a spring-fed pond
Feasting on gnat fry

Through the heat shimmer
Nature's stealth technology
The small falcon drops
Grasps the dragonfly
And retreats from the chalk horse
Confidence intact

Feet of clay

A cuckoo flew to Dartmoor
And schemed along the way
It very soon had sensed a boon
Of victims in the hay

A cuckoo is a space-thief
Or so the lore-folk say
It spots a loon by the lighted moon
And plans a raiding day

A cuckoo makes replacement
And seeks to cause dismay
It drops its spoon by the afternoon
To make the buntings pay

A cuckoo is ambitious
A metamorphic jay
Rules in June with a beak-harpoon
To rival's nestlings slay

A cuckoo is amoral
Free-markets to obey
Playing a tune for any buffoon
With a profit-egg to lay
But,
A cuckoo's not a scoundrel
For anthropomorphic play
No banker's rune or gangster's goon
But a bird with feet of clay

Uneaten

At first glow over the east ridge
The morning star shows its Jekyll face
And a glimpsed form with a deft fox gait
Cuts the crust of frost to a darker space

Venus wanes in the winter dawn
As light-foot shadows leave the chalk slope
To sheltered tangles of bramble cave
With shivered urgency and hidden hope

Later,
Even-star waxes on the west ridge
Where fungal fruits defy the cold
An inkcap waiting in Hyde-form
For fatal physic to unfold

By full night, the creatures resume
The claim on their rightful larder
They step past the withering mushroom
That lies in the moon light uneaten

Green-washed

Riding from Bath to Llangower
A boy scoured the sky without pause
To glimpse a near-mythic forked tail and ponder
The decline of red kites and its cause

Eschewing the monochrome slag-heaps
Above terraces drab and grey walled
The boy fixed his eyes on the green-washed hillsides
And everything else was ignored

Kites were then close to extinction
Confined to small valleys in Wales
By thoughtless casual cruel persecution
And toxic insecticide sales

Now,
After a five-decade care plan
The red buzzard-rival is back
Its confident flight is a daily delight
Though the coal valley's prospects stay stubbornly black

Hanging on wings close to stall speed
The hen kite is scavenging food
Her prehensile tail wraps currents of air
As she drags off dead meat for her brood

The kites now have space and rich pickings
A lobscouse of roadkill and prey
They're now cast in the rural pan-drama
With tacit permission to stay

Will there be long-term commitments
To birds once symbolically rare?
Or will a familiar expedient indifference
Displace all co-operative care?

So,
In places once grey and now green
Late gate-posts of kites' refuge hills
Will meaningful lasting improvements be seen
With promises pledged and fulfilled?

Or,
Could kites be a new Cinderella
When special-case status is gone?
Once again veiled in a shadowy dale
Trapped between gauntlet and gamekeeper's gun?

Rooks claim the city

From perfect nests that never fall
the rooks descend on Cleary Field
And by Darwinian brief affray
They banish rivals, jack and jay
To form a cocky crow-strut shield

With burnished purpose to prevail
And insistent top floor custody
They apply the force of sanctioned greed
Consumption and gain the only creed
That sanctifies their territory

The flock swoops up by instinct
With cliffs of glass and steel behind
To fortunes clearly on the wax
Reflected in thirty Saint Mary Axe
Gifted permanently to their kind

Then,
Drawn to a pond by thirst at dawn
One rook has glimpsed a mirrored world
Looks past reflected self-romance
And narcissistic arrogance
Briefly to see himself unfurled

A fine decree

The birds had gathered one full day
  Across the grain of nature's mix
A truce of predator and prey
Called to court by the king of fowls
Hawks, pigeons and many more
Paid obeisance to the cry

Then transpired a great debate
Of a transforming deep proposal
To ensure all feathered creatures
As posited by a jenny wren
Will have the world at their disposal
Despite genus, species, cock or hen

Every sharp-eyed gaze held fast
Those scions of a saurian past
Until Peregrine by ethereal shriek
Called order for the vote
And parliament made a fine decree
Gifting avian opportunity

Then, a thrum passed through the woods
And, a host of hopeful common birds
With expectations of rebirth
Appeared, it seems by chance
Though truly, only golden-crested wrens
Went skipping to the dance

Slumberjack

Oxbow stands bright in the frost
An auto-amputated remnant of the Avon
The frog-rich favourite of apex birds
Illuminated egret and cloud-blended heron
They seem to reign

Beneath a rime of bullrush ice
A long green fish holds station
Marooned when small by a summer flood
Avoiding avian spears and arrows
Staying secret, grey and dappled
Eating tadpoles, frogs and minnows
And growing

In open-eyed sleep the green fish waits
For food, a mate, another flood
Submerged and subversive, patient and quick
The birds not seeing its hue of mud
One day it darts forward, grasping a leg
An egret pulled under, drowned and devoured
The pike no longer a slumberjack
But the ruler of Oxbow, a king alone

Gene republic

A black wasp left its sandy nest
And over-flew the Queen Ann's lace
Then turned across an oilseed field
Risking the toxic shadow vale
To find a meadow's freedom blooms
A natural, safe, and humble place

Life abounds on the unploughed slopes
Haven for insect refugees
Saved from the drive for cheapened food
They keep the keys for purer times
Meadows are a gene republic
Wholesome islands in the poison seas

A black wasp left its sandy nest
And flew toward an apple stand
It drank sap in a cottage orchard
Ageing trees in a happy space
Gardens preserving habitat
Asylum in the agri-wasteland

Semblances

Mayfly hatching storm
Drifting clouds of semblances
River abundance

Fish rising to feast
A brief instant of plenty
River ambrosia

Tranquil atmosphere
Reed warbler's trilling gargle
River utopia

Appetites declared
Darwinian rules remain
River survival

Woods

Wood music

Secluded in Wistman's near Dartmoor's heart
The pure night hours are almost silent
A nearby stream makes soft trickle-talk
Muting the sounds of cautious movement

A landscape made of forsaken places
Stone rows and hut circles, mines and farms
The soil scratched thin for gold and iron
Now healed by moss and cleansed by storms

Then dawn comes
First, Yaffle drums on a dead dry Ash
Living anew with beetles and lichens
Timing the call when the sky starts to glow
As stars take their leave and sparkle-dew brightens

So, cue April in an English forest
The rustle of leaves, the yelp of a deer
Hundreds of songbirds call out to their kind
An exquisite choir that sings without fear

This is wood music
Transient and perfect but never repeated
Unalloyed joy in an air-carried message
By creatures at home where threats have retreated

Ivy time

High on a hill on Cranborne Chase
A remnant copse of old oaks sits
Amid a pest-free sea of wheat
In quiet sink-holed isolation
An oasis of the wilder world
Unchanged since times candlelit
Wood in tune with saprophytes
Tangled strands in free formation
Bramble, ivy, old man's beard
Refuge for the native strains
Waiting for the wilding time
When diverse life reclaims its station

So, life prevails
Autumn brings busy artisans
To sticky flowers on dark green leaves
They need not wait for prime perfection
The bees have found their ivy time

Mistle

The woods are looming on the ridge
The rain is drifting mistle-thin
With siren sounds now clearly heard
Plain lone birdsong draws you in
The piping-sad hypnotic notes
Evoking lost druidic times
And gifts of oak sperm on the tree
White bull worship and chanted rhymes
The creature's voice rings gorgeously
Seductively erodes freewill
So, eyes towards the treetops turn
To see the singer holding still
Beside its namesake mistletoe
Protector of all Roman life
And within Nemi's golden grove
Diana's shelter from all strife
But for the Trojan Aeneas
It was a life-blood lucky charm
When to Hades he descended
Protected him from demon-harm
And thus, the mistle-magic lives
The pride-proclaiming mistle thrush
With centuries of mystery
Of mistletoe and mistle-hush
The bird might be a harbinger
Of Taranis and the wheeling-shrike
Its warnings come with the rising sun
Like offspring of a lightning strike

Understorey

Dawn comes like a spark to Harnham Slope
The damp ground glittered by the rising sun
Low-angle rays searching the woods
Lighting small worlds of the understorey
That lie unseen, or perhaps unheeded
Like a big idea kept quietly secret

And so, a village came to light
Briefly glimpsed under shady boughs
Carefully crafted in rustic style
By children as an unselfconscious game
Then casually left for fate's determination
Its hopeful perfection never intended to be seen

Listen to the dawn

On a timeless moonlight foot journey along an ancient
chalky trail
A wanderer finds the space of mind to truly listen to the
dawn
The quietly exaggerated rustle of sleekit night folk hiding
And pre-dawn silences when the owls return to roost
At first light the night air becomes restless, and
Through the rim-trees of the old ox drove
A westerly wind makes ridge-music
Sweeping the rook chatter east
Fusing sound with distance
Dispatched to sunrise
Decrescendo
Then the light of all life
Releases a synthesis of colour, sound and scent
And the wayfarer knows for the first time he has heard a day
start

Foragers

Urban fashions, country traditions
Foragers set out
For food for free
It feels like fun
In all conditions
The skills come naturally
Slowly walking
Along a hedge, through a wood
Scanning, spotting, testing, showing
Is that edible, is that good?
Gather berries, gather knowledge
Smelling, smiling, pressing, sharing
Fungus caution, seems instinctive
Learn from mothers, elders, others
Stinking nightshade, inkcap, mandrake
Scary, wary, nary risky
Careful of those found provisions
Blackberry, elder, crab, sloe
All safe, some bitter
Stay alert, careful picking
A metaphor for all decisions
For when,
A forager digs for roots
She finds her core

Dignity

The essence of the churchyard tree
That casts its shade upon the ground
Is dignity not piety
Or so it is, that I have found

Planted to meet a high appeal
To grow the wood to craft the bows
Compounding with whale bone and steel
The fragrant tension of the yews

Then made redundant by firearms
They grew and flourished in repose
To grace the villages and farms
Too old and treasured to depose

With pungent scent and berries bright
The yews provide a mellow sight
So, many timeless trees still stand
With old stone churches on their land

Scented memories

On a cold January day
Brightly dry with a bird-stilling frost
A garden fire sent seep-smoke
Through the sun-halo of clematis seed
Climbing on the old apple trunk
To perfume the morning and evoke
A cascade of scented memories

Fragrance drifting in faint mist
Slow-burn bramble and orchard twigs
English incense for a mistletoe mystery
Released by fire from native sprigs
Smells from deep in species history
Age-affirming, place-confirming
A seductive compass for contentment

Ashmore Wood

A shmore Wood
April in a tense year
Sun spears light the ground
Perfect anemones now abound
Prim-flowers fading as we clearly hear
The nuthatch piping and the kite's thin call

Wormwood
April in a lethal year
Wildfires light the ground
Imperfect creatures scurry around
Bitter flowers thrive through a time of fear
Of heartless sniping while the dumb bombs fall

Ashmore Wood
Year-renewing source
Later blooms come into force
The carpet now is yellow and blue
With a poignant mix of colours now due
To enlighten the walk to a serene place for all

Deadwood

Old oak stump
City of wood wasps
Kept alive

Tall oak stump
Woodpecker larder
Chicks survive

Fallen stump
Mosses and fungi
Spore and thrive

Dead wood world
From which new lifeblood
Will derive

Fallen tree

In lightless caverns of chalky water deep roots drink
The chemical-craft of small sightless ancient creatures
Claimed from the mysterious half-known rocky features
Of the windless limestone under-world
Old water for an old tree in a seeming timeless silence,
     locked away
Restless water, sentence-served, seeking now a spring
Eager for the surface-world and the freedom it will bring

The surface has been storm-swept by dark and howling
     soughs
And furious wind and water have felled the aged tree
Lying in the aftermath on its cracked and broken boughs
It appears to be the certain end of arboreal dignity

But that was ten years in the past
A robust branch had cracked the stone above the hidden
     stream
A new-formed pond now teems with life, its water liberated
Filled and kept by a nascent spring that was an abstract
     dream
And the tree is the slowly crumbling home of many lucky
     lives
Beetles, birds and fungi, wasps and bees and mice
So, when seen in early evening it seems a tragedy
Then by sunset light one comes to see the beauty of a fallen
     tree

Wood land

Far from any road
A hopeful woodland
By gradual organic change
And light touches by its keepers
Comes to reincarnate the original forest
That gifted space and fire to the post-glacial Britons
And despite
The post-industrial
Contemptuously replete
Fly-tippers who enter the trees
To creep up, and along with the detritus
Dump their decency and dignity on the bridlepath
There will be
Over geological time
By patient biological quanta
And consequent redressing degrees
A time when the bones of the gluttonous
Gift space and water to the post-Anthropocene trees

Mistleberry Wood

Approached from its south side
The composite sound of Mistleberry Wood
Is calm and mellow and best understood
Through children's joy to run and hide
In the shadows of the tree-claimed prehistoric fort

The erstwhile clash of arms
And roar and din of territorial war
Are long consigned to legend and lore
Replaced by hen wren's calls of alarm
And the purest notes of a blackbird in full voice

Iron-age ancestors
Might lament the overleaped banks
But we enjoy the steepened flanks
Now a home for springtime nestlings
A hilltop haven for creatures wild and free

Water

The Corner

1963
With friends
Long hot summer
Many sultry fishing days
Smokey sundown camp fires
Spawned our hard-held ownership
Of the deep scoured bend in the river
A watery wall-bound enclave called The Corner
That was our place, our peace, our hearth and our legend

Once
Rivals arrived
Demanded to fish
The river between us
Displays of cowboy swagger
Insults we learned from war films
First stones thrown to splash the water
Then more stones thrown to hurt each other
Tired, cut and bruised but no ground conceded
Home for tea, and the irony of bread poppy-seeded
Soon enough we dispersed to new schools and alliances
And the spell of The Corner and its uncelebrated battle receded

Forbidden craft

Tired of the small fish in the brook
We built a boat of planks and drums
To liberate, like Tom and Huck
Boys to bigger better waters
Fed by our small rejected stream

The raft was our blood-sworn keepsake
Forbidden craft, forbidding place
Moored on the dark echo-still lake
Known in undertones as Rock Pond
A no-go no-fishing abyss

We fished for that for which we yearned
A verified catch of hunter status
Elusive giant pike and eels
Would to the angling summit take us
With satisfaction and content

But the lake had only brook-fish
So, we lost our concentration
Drifting through shadows and half-light
Where in fisher-floating silence
We came upon an awe-inspiring sight

As one we felt the import of our sensual discovery
When mythic tales transformed to become a clear reality
We brightly saw and felt the mysterious enjoyment
Of teenage lovers tangled on a hidden mossy bank
Their urgent movements seeding both our shock and
    aspiration
As the primary place of fishing in our waking dream-world
    sank

Wet fly sinking

A trout by half glimpse
Then, a perfect whisper cast
Fly line symmetry

Many fishing days
In this flowing chalk bed stream
Might make a savant

What is the reward?
For river supplication
And time invested

Surely, to see through
A brief sun-gate in the cloud
The wet fly sinking

Last cast

Time of high portent
Autumn spider-web morning
Dawn dew-nets glisten

Such a pious place
Subservient to the light
An old spring-fed lake

Cold watery air
A soupy arc of the line
First cast of the fly

Connected fisher
Understanding seeping in
Last cast approaches

Grayling rise

Clear water riffling
Early morning grayling rise
Fish time instinctive

Casting many hours
Enter the waterside trance
Real time receding

Evening sun-fall
Insects reflect the low light
Real time contracting

Last cast at sunset
Perfect but ineffective
Real time resuming

Cyclonic future

Another storm overfeeds the catchment
So, rivers rise beyond the heron's table
Gardens flood with leech-laced mud
And inundations cease to be a fable

Slipping from our interglacial niche
We create a fickle steamy nature
Burn substrates with profligate abandon
Then adapt to a more cyclonic future

Or, we could be
Pleading for living slower and lighter
Winding down the hydrocarbon plunder
Seeing warning in the water's need to swell
And heeding the electric voice of thunder

Weather forecast

The forecast is a mirror of consequences
Of lives objectively absurd
Consumption trumps replacement
Of the end-game
Scarce a word
Production outgrows clearance
Heads in the sand
Storms not heard

An overburdened biosphere
Unplugged at Holocene pace
Means very rugged adjustments
Will take place
The runners of correction
Are already here
With frequent inundations
While other places parch
So,
The Reckoner howls in from the West
To settle a debt by the Ides of March

In a riverine state

Along the gurgle-world of a brook bank
Impossibly clear water leads minds to take stock
Of the apparent permanence of gravel and block
And the natural perfection of a Wiltshire chalk stream

We retreat to this triumph of heart over head
The seductive reassurance of geological time
Ignore the upheaval that once formed the lime
The ooze-stone laid down in ancestral seas

But despite this forgivable forever view
The carbon-march has picked up speed
Liberated by Anthropocene greed
So, the stones will change

Meanwhile,
Walking and dreaming by a stream in spate
A hint of the everlasting in its sound and scent
Fostering a hope for a future equilibrium
And settling the spirit in a riverine state

Places

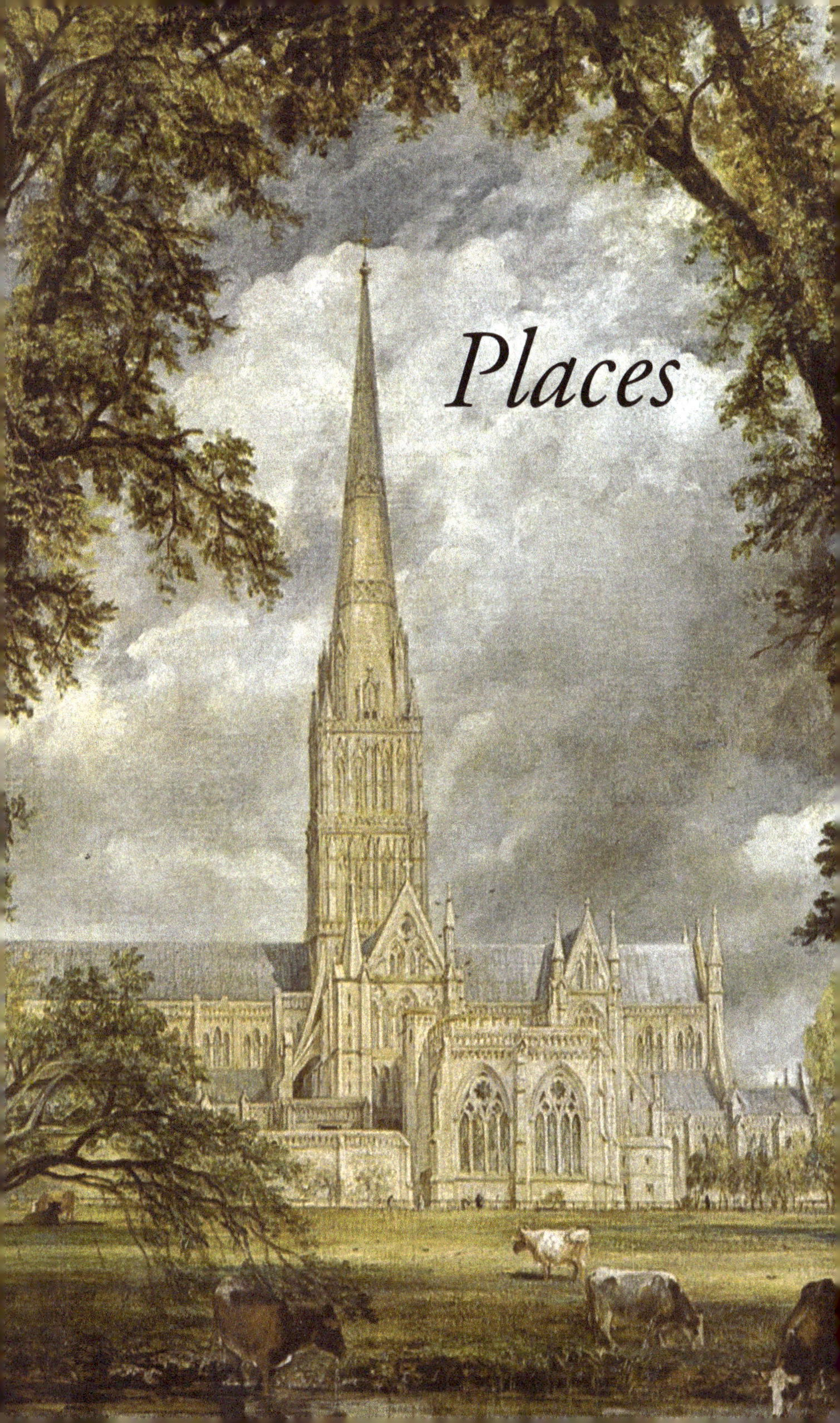

Chalk pit

By the beginning of bat light
The old chalk pit donates its heat
And children stay behind to play
With cries of daring and freedom
While robins sing a dusk lament
For nightingales no longer heard

The quarry may have sent its stone
To feed the hungry limekiln's fire
But by that loss, and healed by time
Has slowly come to be replaced
Making a warm and tangled space
Where nature's creatures feel at home

So, time-renewed, it might one day
Welcome a nightingale's return
And hear again the midnight song
Approve the children's precious voice
Such a prodigal use of rock
Could be a fresh Luscinia's choice

Stilling henge

Just before the evening owl-dark falls
A movement is caught in a stilling henge
Along with a sound that starts and stalls
Rhythmic chanting, benightment to avenge

A child skips around the looming blocks
Counting off shadows in the dropping sun
Finding core numbers that light up the rocks
Radians, planes and angles, all as one

She searches for a history-solving sign
So, when her quick-brain abstract thinking hones
Will she be the wrangler who can define
The geometric secrets of the stones?

Or, like many have sensed in times before
See the stones of Avebury promise more

Time entombed

Trees stand guard
Within the special stones
Ancient space

Bones taken
Reverence assured
Time entombed

Deserted
Grassy spirit-sea
Lark vigil

Survival
The stones radiate
Influence

Drove

Ancient ridgeway droves
Were conduits for cattle
Millions of hooves

Cows crossing the road
In cars we wait patiently
Like them, nose to tail

The herd-speed is fixed
Has been so for centuries
A law of nature

The drover once walked
Now rides a muddy quadbike
But moves no faster

Heathland safari

Silence at midday
Start the heathland safari
Searching for reptiles

Sun-warmed sand patch
Ideal for scaly creatures
No lizard basking

Looking in the ferns
A half-apparent grass snake
Was a green cable

Sceptical party
Losing faith in the leader
Cell phones come to life

Saved by the car park
Two adders watch each other
On the hot tarmac

Field walls

Moss suits an ageing wall
Lichen perfects the flint and brick
Hands that made it long since passed
Never to see its time-rendered beauty

Dry stones stacked to fence a field
Seem to mark a spread cathedral
Shaping, enclosing and sustaining
An illusion of rural permanence

A meadow

L ove labour
 Friends make a meadow
Creative

Twenty years
To change the grasses
With patience

Comes alive
With native insects
Returning

Bequeathing
A deeper future
Securely

Cathedral Close

Winter sun and frost
  Create our gracile shadows
On the sleeping grass

Leafless willows stand
Tall gamines of their genus
Near the ancient yews

Autumn's rotting leaves
Return to earth by worm-pull
To arise renewed

A dove is calling
Bringing thoughts of another
Faraway garden

Stained

Westerly sunlight
Flooding the stained glass
Ancient numinous

Expectant chatter
Echoing throughout the nave
Orchestra tuning

Conditioned church-hush
The choir rises to begin
Anticipation

Intense waves of sound
Gerontius's step-dream
Beyond space and time

Completely absorbed
We join him through his judgement
Solemn, hopeful, then joyous
Finally peaceful

Vanishing point

Crossing the ridgeway in patchy spring sunlight
Settled In the rhythmic calm of a walker's meditation
The day was instantly and briefly given to parallels
Ploughed furrows, power cables, aeroplane contrails
Modern road, the mysterious cursus, Roman pavement
For a moment all inclined to an identical vanishing point
A fleeting physical metaphor of common purpose
Then, the vision was lost, its appearance fortuitous
And a happy irregularity reclaimed the landscape
The haphazard freewill of people, plants and animals
With no false notion of destiny

Favoured place

The White Hart pub at Castle Combe became a favoured
place
A crowd of us had gathered there again
For spontaneous farewell drinks before dispersal
But elevated spirits could not hide a growing trace
Of sadness and regret among the friends
Who felt, deep down, that this was no rehearsal

Of all the lissom girls those days there was a special one
I hoped to hold in quiet conversation
But the room was packed with laughter, smoke and noise
So, we left the raucous party to see the setting sun
At last, to slowly walk and softly talk
As I admired her honey hair and poise

Through the mossy Cotswold lanes, we reached the highest
rise
Exchanging views on many varied topics
Until I grew a clear and shakeless view
The girl with perfect willowy form and serious hooded eyes
Might agree to be an intimate love-long friend
To share and make with me a life and family too

Stories

Assimilation

From his vantage point
A lean nut-brown blue-eyed man
Watches the trees cut clear

The crash of timber
Flays his Mesolithic heart
He senses an ending

Diminished hunting
Constricted foraging land
Falling to the flint

He will keep his bow
Will not kneel before the hoe
For the dawning age
He intuitively knows
Defies resistance
And so, his daughter's daughter
Will wed a farmer

Axe heads

A warrior of the early bronze age
Hid a precious axe in a shallow pit
Then was, despite a fierce indignant rage
Overcome by raiders for want of it

And there it lay below a leather shield
Exerting no influence while resting
Until it bent a brief magnetic field
And was prised from its chalk and clay bedding

Now polished, the ancient metal weapon
Has fallen into ownership again
Just another object, honour undone
Within the Cathedral Close to remain

Meanwhile, in a dusty derelict shed
A rough neglected wrought-steel axe was found
The worm-drilled shaft fell away from the head
To reveal a farm-tool, rusty but sound

The finder saw something unusual
In its perfectly smithed balance and form
So, off to seek an expert's perusal
He walked it through the crooked streets of Frome

Now both axe-heads in fine museums lay
Four thousand years and thirty miles apart
They look the same as on their forging-day
Though fixed display has robbed them of their heart

Diminished

A body buried
To leave lasting memory
Seeding a legend

The spirit was lost
Nullified by Roman rule
Never seen again

Barrow spread thinly
A sacrifice to farming
Saxon-perfect fields

Swept by wind and time
The dolmen stands denuded
A diminished grave

Roman bones

Looking across the chalk hills at sunset
Our star is in its most revealing form
Pointing up soil-scribbles of history
From the time-faded Celts to modern farms
Tempting us to assume predestiny
In the current peaceful fertile land and
Find pride in our classic antiquity
Villas, spas and mosaics we admire
Military codes to which we aspire
Scoured by the memory-lens of modernity

But there was a price for Pax Romana
Eclipsing the barrow-building Britons
With lasting suppression of mystic thought
And straight roads paving the way for dogma
So, despite much change that others brought
The Saxons, Angles, Danes and Normans
And new blood from Britannia's roaming
Our brains still rattle with italic bones
And eclectic British genomes not withstanding
We remain in deeper essence Romans

The rime of a Sarisberie masoun

1220

A wery masoun, drynketh on his bed
Tok reste, that made hym to slepe faste
And he dremeth how to kep hys bairns fed
Hys duty fulfyld and mette at laste
With werke gan wexen as in the paste
Pardieux, bye dwellynge in another place
To serve his folk and God in al his grace

As he met thoght weel in the long derke nyght
A voice telleth of a plan heard mencioun
For on olde feldes, in a place ful of lighte
To bylde a fyne cherche of grete dimencioun
With hette nede for a sickerly masoun.
So, comen swiftly to that place so deere
Be ful of blysse with your conscience clere

By nexte day he tok leave of his gud wyfe
With hed enclyned and with ful humble cheere
And gan hym forth with ne tyme for stryfe
Tyme to make, not taryinge lengere here
Afore faylen lyte, Sarisberie was neer
So, he to swich a rightful place shulde wende
And fynde gud werke to last withouten ende

A gardyn he aspyed betwix the stremes
Upon a river, in a cool grene mede
And many oke and hardy asshe for bemes
With felde floures blewe, yelwe, white and rede
All ravyshyng swetnesse, and nothyng dede
The water swymmen ful of fishes lighte
With fynnes rede and skales sylver bryghte

Swich place he was astoned to beholde
There wexe ek every holsom floure and gras
On blosmy bows he herde the byrdes synge bolde
So attempre a toun as ever was
To fynd oon better nevere com to pas
No man upon gan ther waxe sek ne old
Or to suffer a grevaunce hot ne cold

Byfore, with the day waxen swiftly derke
He gan fynde the maistre masoun spekyng
Freinen hym beren oon moore soul mak werke
On the grete ston cherche with sicker connyng
As al hys lyf he was so bethynkyng
To which he wrought so wel to hys pleasaunce
That to hym ought to ben a sufficaunce

Quod he "I graunte it yow", and right anon
This formel maistre spak in this degree:
"A myghty cherche, afore thys yer be gon,
Will theen by masouns werken skylfully,
So whanne sterten is for youre choys al fre,
So, with this werde ne tary lengere heere
As I seyed thus ye have assuren fere"

1230
Ten yers after Bishop Poore's stonding ston
   The gud cherche wals risen at ful swithe pase
This al and som the masoun's werke was don
With happi herte ne toilen in thys place
And whoso may at tyme have swiche grace
Werken heere and be besekynge ful servyse
For ani masoun wit moore can suffyse

His wyfe to Sarisberie comen wight
Truly he was ne a smal-swivinge man
She was hys swetnesse and he here lyght knight
And here love he was joien for ed-gan
This is no feyned mater I tellen can
In al dayes in here servise he wuld dye
But grace be, myght it never com therebye

Thys werke by hevenysh revolucioun
Bryngeth the masoun fortune truly wel
The cherche hath take hym in subjecccioun
But, fyndeth hym dignite to fair tel
With hys wife and familie in gud sel
Maketh hys thoght in joy and blis habounde
So curtaysly forth-gon, werke nat confounde

1250
Ful thriti yers by hys hond-craft liven
And nevere oon tyme nede for bred beggen
Thys place in lyf for he what gan striven
By wys discrecioun in thys toun biggen
What wonder ys it, to fynd it yeven
Taylage for hys sone, yet no tyrannye
Humblesse and pees, gud feith, prosperite

More yers paas with gud tyme gan renen
The masoun ne werke, so feble he wex
Ther was no more but unto bed geinen
Oon nyte he swelte as he lay on the flex
His wyf bicomen on harken hys yex
She recheth hys shete at myghty ful spede
Oon quik glenten and she cleped hym dede

The crafty masoun who bilden the sete
In hys poure grave unsolempne slepen
Bishops aplenty gin nempnen replete
While the feithful masouns rare be-mynen
Shall he compleyne unto God a-trien?
No, for ston he salueth and wyth chere
Hys familie holden as frends ful dere

Legacy

Close to a hamlet in Tudor times
A settled field in Wiltshire stood
Allotted land with informal title
A worked and cherished source of food
In summer loved and in winter vital

But this bucolic idyll was soon to cease
The landlord had a brutal vision
To cleanse all peasants from his view
And treating them with cruel derision
His henchmen slaughtered all but a few

Thereby, the roughest earl prevailed
His landscape now serene and pure
And, with despotic greed and lack of grace
He vainly gazed, himself to assure
An empty heart in a plentiful place

Now, we think with keener retrospection
Despite the smoky lens of history
And sentimental stories that some recall
In this tale there is no mystery
The grandee was the greatest grobian of them all

Singing began

First there was fire, then there was stone
Wetness began, stone became bone
Then became us, woman and man
Life was lighted, singing began

Chanting the fireside baby's new bones
Lauding the strength of youths in their prime
Blackbird fluting the egg-bones of life
Every bone-song comes at its time

The symphonic clatter, deep in the past
Bone turning slowly to stone once again
The saurian music silent at last
Succeeded by Mistle's haunting refrain

We sing new dead bones into the earth
In graveyard, barrow, ash-urn or clay
Rightfully resting and turning to stone
Where they belong and where they should stay

Eggbox

As dusk was falling in the dell
Small birds were ticking in alarm
And clear day left and clear night fell
'til the spirit of the deep still dark
Seeped the harsh Victorian Downs

A vagrant of those ragged times
Craved shelter from the midnight chill
And by luck-light found a barrow-cave
Mysterious dolmens standing still
Steadfast in the faltered heaves of fate

His eyes perceived an entry-word
So boldly scratched above the door
He sensed uncommon welcome
Inviting, warm, kind and wholesome
Drawing him in and promising more

Weary from his wandering life
The straw-floor seemed a fortune-bed
A perfect peaceful place to rest
To drink some wine and take the bread
That kept him from the cavern of despair

He once had been an army man
Captain of a military camp
But by one dice-call and a duelling ball
Lost family, commission, respect and all
And became a wandering tramp

He drifted like the curling smoke
That rose up from his glowing bowl
Until with uncanny awareness
He sighted a deep stone hole
And was drawn like a bat to its darkness

In that ancient lithic niche
A neat wooden box was encased
It possessed a tangible aura
Like a reliquary purposely placed
That demanded its contents be faced

The tramp took hold with a greedy grip
Then flipped the dry lid open
And by lost light in that stone-age grave
He saw the message, sharp, bespoken
For him alone, his future to save

In the box were six small eggs
From sundry song birds stolen
Ever nestled in wool-scraps dry
For these poor birds would never fly
Or sing for kindred, free and open

At once the vagrant saw the truth
To him was the eggbox speaking
For he had taken eggs and lives
By impetuous thoughtless wreaking
And as boy and man, risk and greed
Became his self-destructive need
Until the pistol crack was heard
And his life changed in an inkling

His mind was touched by rare relief
And a deep sleep overcame him
His dreams were bright with new belief
That atonement for a past so grim
Was a duty that must begin
With the eggbox and the jewels therein

At dawn he took the box outside
To better see its contents
But all he saw was six lead balls
And pondered on their portent
Then,
A blackbird sang, a robin too
The spirit of the eggs came through
Clarifying his onward way
To forgive himself for all his deeds
And set aside his pride-fed needs
For to live again a freed-man

Sarum-bound

In Hardy's time when travel was by horse or foot
A weary walker stopped to rest on Pentridge Knoll by Martin
Down
He drifted into sleep amid the ancient chieftains' graves
And lay in utter stillness on a hand-made wool rug, deftly
thrown
He sighed as stone-age forebears visited his dream
Lamenting loss of old flint-skills for shaping wood and horn
From the peaceful fruitful cursus-path that megaliths adorn
To burning stones in wasteful fires to see the metals gleam
Then, ambassadors of bronze and iron joined his reverie
With tales of earthen-works and forts, and tribal rivalry
And Caesar's builders of the roads that changed all memory

Suddenly, the walker was woken by a fox's howl
Alarmed by the sound, and then by the silent night
The dream was fresh, the ghosts seemed at hand
But the traveller had no need to fear the barrow-wight
It was a peaceful dark with harmless living creatures on the prowl
And benign spirits of the past who understood the precious land

At dawn he resumed his task, Sarum-bound
Descended from his sleeping-mound to the antique Roman dyke
Above, a flock of rooks flew west with a raucous crow-cry sound
And as his chess-piece dream-folk faded
First, he lost count of the rooks,
Then, he lost sight of the rooks
And finally forgot the rooks
As he walked into the city at midday

Plunder

A landed man proclaimed himself a servant of the time
But nonetheless held title over every creature's season
And when subtly cross-questioned about this role sublime
He retreated into sophistry and self-enlightened reason
It was a holy burden, he said, to maintain the great estate
Handed down from times of yore, in which he had no choice
A simple quirk of birth right, a weary twist of fate
Contrived by misty ancestors, an echo of their voice

Then one day when shooting, he wandered through a wood
Keeping faith with duty, to thin the rooks in number
He came upon a barrow-ghost enrobed in cloak and hood
So surely, he must be dreaming and should awake from
    slumber

Quietly, the apparition spoke,
"I was long here when your forebear received his bosky
    plunder
You cannot atone on bended knee with a rosary to fumble
So, supplicate to Nature and do it with wide wonder
And be careful not to try too hard to be so falsely humble
Accept your transient power and enjoy it in full measure
As the day will surely come when another takes your
    treasure"

Venison

The platform lends line of sight
With treasured gun balanced clear
A man waits for dawn
He waits through the night
He waits for Roe deer
Venison as a sacrifice

In his settled vigil-seat
He dreams of dressing the carcass
Giving respect by ritual movement
Hooded in the stalker's cowl
A mummer to the meat
Venison as a sacrament

With Venus on the rise
A doe and fawn emerge from cover
He waits for the stag
Only from discipline and convention
His primaeval heart to smother
Venison as a social test

The stag is barely visible
The gun is kept on hold
No clear shot is possible
So, he climbs down the ladder
With a hunter's coded humility
Venison as a moral artifice

Incredulous

At the age of ten, or thereabouts
When fishing on the Boyd
I saw a white stoat in July
In all its ermine glory
It made no effort to avoid
My brief incredulous gaze
And thus, began of a story
That nobody believed
Of a giant river weasel-ghost
"Jake, you lying swede"

The more I insisted upon
The veracity of my tale
The greater was the scorn
That scorched within my pale
And so, I gleaned an essence
That has served me ever since
To muster proper evidence
If I'm seeking to convince
And, an exaggerated telling
Is a detractor's perfect gift
So, tell it straight and tell it true
Or keep it for a later shift
Don't pander to a rival's grift

Firestone

Uplifted in a freshly ploughed field
The flint was a perfect shape
Like a bone at first glance
Until a cracked edge
Caught a misty glint in the early sun
Declaring its firestone nature
And laying claim to a prodigious mineral influence
Blade, axe, arrowhead, spark liberator
The primary tool-stone for millennia
Only iron seemed truly better
Bronze merely a transition
So surely, it was iron that startled Pandora
When the jar was opened
Releasing Vulcan-craft upon the world
And the promethean fire-decline began
Forging, scurrying, globalizing, weaponizing
Faster and hotter, then involuting
Perhaps the time is sweeping in
When someone might start again with flint

Release

A pervading air of lamentation
For many plague-lost friendships can befall
Those who submit to a hesitation
When release is sanctioned from The Hall
So,
A spring-hungry lass, with concentration
Followed a briar-wrapped old stone wall
Searching the margin of a pine plantation
For a flushing green and a coal tit's call
The hawthorn was paused in bud formation
A Northeast wind made the first growth stall
But the bright dawn brought illumination
Radiant warmth to make the fog-ice fall
Feeling this was winter's termination
The woman stood straighter, spritely and tall
Believing with some determination
In better days approaching, after all